Astrology

The Planets, Elements, Zodiac Signs, and How They Affect Your Life

By Samantha Scott

Published in Canada

© Copyright 2015 –Samantha Scott

ISBN-13: 978-1515180968
ISBN-10: 1515180964

Table of Contents

Why Do People Believe?

Why do people hold onto any superstitious or supernatural beliefs? As it relates to astrology, people choose to believe because it gives them a lot of desirable information about their lives, and the way that the future will unravel. It offers tangible ways to resolve problems, and to work at improving their relationships with family, friends, and romantic interests. The way that people use astrology these days, can bring a lot of joy and satisfaction. When people read their horoscopes, it gives them more control over their own destiny, and causes them to feel satisfied and happy. Astrologers will not always get every specific detail right, about all of the people who fall under a certain sign.

However, reading your horoscope can provide valuable insights, and help in many ways. In order to truly benefit from a reading, you must have someone create a personal natal chart for you. Followers of astrology do not believe that things in life happen just by coincidence. Instead, they believe that things occur for very good reasons. You can use astrology to find the answers to questions, about why things happen, or what is going to happen in the future. This is why so many people choose to use astrology in their lives, in order to help them better understand the world around them.

Chapter 1:
Basics of Astrology

Astrology is basically the art of observing how the other plants relate with the Earth. Please remember that in order to make things easier to follow, astrologers refer to the sun and moon as planets, even though they're not really. From this point forth, when this book refers to the "planets", the sun and moon are included.

Each of the planets represents an energy that makes up people's very beings. These include things like feelings, love, and how people communicate. As well as affecting these things, the position of the planets in the sky also shows observers what style the elements are in at any time.

As it relates to star sings and horoscopes, the positions the planets were in at the moment of a person's birth, alters how the planets affect the rest of their life.

Astrologers have separated the skies into 12 different areas, and used them to create 12 archetypes. These are what people know as the zodiac signs today.

There are **fours basic aspects** involved in astrology: **the houses**, **the planets**, **the zodiac signs**, and **the aspects**.

Astrology uses the view of the celestial bodies in the sky, as seen from Earth. From this point, they appear to be orbiting around us here. This works well for the purposes of astrology, since it's about viewing the interactions of the Earth with the rest of the universe.

While the planets orbit the sun, they travel through the positions of the 12 different zodiac signs. The sun goes through a different sign every month, and then starts the cycle again once per year. This period is actually what gives people on Earth the very concept of "years". However, the moon will go through all 12 zodiac signs each month. "Month" actually comes from a word that means "moon".

You can then see how the whole idea of months and years, which affect our lives every day, are closely tied in with the celestial cycles, and the zodiac signs. This goes way back into ancient times, when all of these things were observed with painstaking care.

Since the path the planets move through is seen to be flat, it's possible to draw it in two dimensions. This is done by drawing a circle, and then dividing it into 12 sections, like a big, galactic pizza. Each one of these sections represents one of the 12 different zodiac signs. The section that each sign falls within relates to where they actually are in the cosmos.

As the planets move around, and their positions change in relation to each other, these are called different "aspects". When there is a high degree of separation between them, they are in "major aspect". Otherwise, they are in "minor aspect". The planets have changing relationships with each other, and those aspects are carefully studies by astrologers. The aspects are actually the key factor that decides whether the energy from a planet flows easily through different individuals, or with difficulty. Think of the power in which these energies flow as being either negative or positive.

These days, astrologers tend to focus on how the different aspects can affect people in positive ways. They believe that they can always be used in some constructive way, no matter what the positions of the planets. If it weren't for the changing aspects, there wouldn't be much to learn from astrology. Things would be still and "silent", without any expressions to read from.

In order to organize their observations, astrologers create charts that detail the things mentioned above. These astrology charts are basically maps of the heavens, taken from one specific time. You will know these observations as "horoscopes". These are usually draw up so that they relate to people's birth dates today. However, in the past, they were typically created for big events, like festivals, times of war, and the crownings of royalty. Long ago, specific charts would only have been created for important people, like kings and queens. These days, as you know, it's easy for anyone to have one drawn for them.

Many know them as horoscopes, but these charts are also called "natal charts". Devotees of astrology tend to shy away from the term "horoscope", because it has been given lower value, by people creating cheap and inaccurate daily predictions for things like newspapers and magazines. In fact, a natal chart can't be properly made for someone, without details about the time of their birth, the date, and place.

If you have one made by an astrologer, you will learn to treasure your chart, as it's the most important thing for anyone who follows astrology. Rather than using words, astrologers use glyphs on charts. These are symbols, and it's easier to use them for quick reference, instead of writing all over a chart.

Chapter 2:
The Four Elements

Every one of the 12 zodiac signs has an element that it falls under: water, fire, earth, and air. They each represent one of the primary forms of energy, and all four of them are present in every person. Through the use of astrology, you can learn how to direct these energies, so that you can better understand how to use your positive traits, and lessen your negative ones.

The different elements are tied to unique types of personalities. Below are detailed explanations about each of the elements.

Water

People with water signs tend to be more sensitive and emotional than others. They are very tuned in with other people, but can themselves be very mysterious. You can think of this in the way that the ocean is vast, quickly changing, and very hard to fully understand. They also have superb memories, enjoy deep conversations, and want to be intimate with other people. In addition, they are eager to provide support to those they love, and willing to criticize themselves openly.

Fire

Fire signs are very temperamental, passionate, and have dynamic personalities. They might have relatively short tempers, which can burn very hot like fire, but will also easily forgive others. They have a strong yearning for adventure and discovery, and have the energy to match. Physically speaking, they are strong. They are usually inspirational to other people as well. They are highly aware of themselves, intelligent, and creative. They have strong ideals, and believe that things can be improved. When it's time to get things done, and move into action, those with fire signs are generally willing.

Earth

These are the more down-to-earth people, who are typically responsible for helping others remain "grounded" in their own lives. They tend to be more realistic about the world, and can also be relatively conservative. People with earth signs can be quite emotional, but not as much so as those with water sign. They enjoy material possessions and having luxuries. They will stand by their friends and families through tough times, are loyal, and also stable.

Air

People who have air signs treasure their relationships with others, and enjoy communicating. They're friendly, smart, analytical types, who love to think about things. They enjoy having deep discussions about philosophical matters, going to social meetings, and also enjoy reading. While they can have a tendency to be pretty superficial, they do like to give people advice.

Chapter 3:
The Zodiac Signs

Would you like to find out more about your own star sign, and how it effects your life and interactions with other people? You are reading just the right book then! The following section will teach you more about the zodiac star signs, the different dates of each of them, and how they are compatible with each other. You will learn about the attributes of each zodiac sign, and how they deal with life, family, and romance.

By looking at the imagery in the sky, as well as the positions of the planets when people were born, astrology can be used to show the fundamental characteristics of different people, as well as their fears, personal flaws, and the things they like. If you find out more about a person's zodiac sign, you can really learn a lot more about them.

In total, there are 12 different zodiac signs. Each one of them has its own strengths, as well as weaknesses. In addition, there are different traits that make each one unique. People of various signs will have specific attitudes and desires that relate to the world around them, as well as the people in it.

Aquarius

Birth date range: January 21 - February 18
Element: Air
Planet: Uranus
Compatibility: Gemini, Libra
Partnerships and marriage: Leo

People born under the Aquarius sign are quiet and shy. However, they can still have a high amount of energy, and be quite eccentric. Whatever type of person they are, they will be smart, deep thinking, and eager to help those in need. They can see things objectively, without allowing prejudices to blur their views. That means there are good at solving problems. They need to have some time alone, on a regular basis, where they can be away from everything else. Even so, they are able to adapt to the energies that surround them, even when not allowed to have their special alone time.

Their power will eventually need to be restored, by being alone, however. Aquarius is ruled by the planet Uranus, with a nature that varies from timid, to more abrupt, and even at times aggressive. This can give an Aquarius an almost visionary type of ability. They are good at understanding what might come in the future, and planning for what they wish to do several years from now. Uranus also allows them to transform quickly, and with little difficulty. That is linked to why they are such good thinkers, and are progressive with their world views.

Friends and Family

They are happy as part of a community, and will always work to be around groups. One of the largest problems faced by those born under Aquarius, is feeling that they're being limited, or held back. They want everyone to be equal, and with freedom. This is why they also want to ensure their own freedom, in what they can say, and what they can do. Other signs view the Aquarius-born as being insensitive, but this is just a wall they put up, to protect against early intimacy with people. Before they can properly express their emotions, they need to be given time to develop trust with others.

Love and Sex

An Aquarius is romantically stimulated the most by intelligence. They will be most likely to desire those who they can have interesting discussions with. Being imaginative, open, willing to take risks, and good at communication, are things that will attract an Aquarius. If you want to have a lasting relationship with one, honesty and integrity is essential. They're not possessive at all, but are committed and loyal.

Pisces

Birth date range: February 19 - March 20
Element: Water
Planet: Neptune
Compatibility: Cancer, Scorpio
Partnerships and marriage: Virgo

Pisces will often keep the company of people who are different from themselves, because they are so friendly. They're quick to help others, and don't look for anything in return. This is due to their selfless nature. As a water sign, they tend to have a high capacity for emotion, as well as empathy. Neptune is their ruling planet, so they're talented at art, and intuitive. This planet is also linked with music, so Pisces-born will enjoy music right from the start of their lives. They're compassionate, generous, caring, and very faithful.

Those who are born under Pisces understand the life cycle intuitively. This means that they also develop the best relationships with other living beings, on an emotional level at least. They are well known for their wisdom. However, when under Uranus' influence, they might become a martyr, to get attention. They're forgiving, and have the most tolerance of any of the signs.

Friends and Family

Since they're so caring and gentle, they can be some of the best friends in the world. They will tend to put what their friends need above their own needs. They're devoted, loyal, and show compassion to any friends or family members who have problems. They're open with their own feelings, but also expect others to act in the same way.

Love and Sex

People born under Pisces are very romantic. They're gentle, loyal, and show expansive generosity to partners. They're also passionate as lovers, and must feel a deep connection in the bedroom. They are not put off by romantic adventures, or shorter relationships. However, they are still immensely loyal when in a relationship.

Aries

Birth date range: March 21 - April 29
Element: Fire
Planet: Mars
Compatibility: Leo, Sagittarius
Partnerships and marriage: Libra

This is the first zodiac sign, and it usually signals the start of something turbulent and energetic. Aries-born are constantly looking for things with speed, dynamics, and a sense of competition. They are the first to be in everything, including social events, or work. With Mars as the ruling planet, Aries are among the most active on the signs. Those born under Aries are there to signify the search for big metaphysical and personal questions, and this is their primary feature.

As a fire sign, they often leap into action, even if that means they've given little thought before hand. They have great organizational skills, and will take on many tasks at a time, and usually finish them quickly. They tend to become angry and frustrated, and can take this out on other people. While they're fiery and focused, they still use their heads to guide them. No matter how old they are, they have a youthful type of energy and strength.

Friends and Family

They are always moving, so they will seek out as many friends as possible. The more different each friend is, the happier an Aries will be. They need to have many personality types in their friends group, in order to be content. This is easy for them to achieve, since they're great at starting communications with others.

Love and Sex

As a fire sign, they enjoy flirting, and making the first move in love. They are happy to tell someone that they're in love with them, as soon as possible. They might do this without thinking about it much before hand. An Aries will show lots of affection, and possibly even too much. They're adventurous, energetic, and passionate, craving passion and sex. These things are all necessary for an Aries to be happy with a relationship.

Taurus

Birth date range: April 20 - May 20
Element: Earth
Planet: Venus
Compatibility: Virgo, Capricorn
Partnerships and marriage: Scorpio

Taurus-born are reliable and strong. They enjoy things that are beautiful and good, and will often surround themselves with material items that bring pleasure. They enjoy tactile and sensual things. Touch is considered very important to them, especially in romance or business. They're conservative and the most reliable sign of all. However, stubbornness is one of their main traits.

Being an earth sign, those born under the sign of the Taurus can be very protective of people they care about. They're good at earning money, and will not give up on projects before finishing them. The symbol of the bull is usually used to indicate stubbornness, but also commitment to getting things done.

Venus is their ruling planet, and it represents beauty, attraction, love, and creativity. This makes them more likely to be great artists, entertainers, or cooks. A Taurus will be loyal, and resistant to unwanted or sudden changes. Out of all the zodiac signs, they are the most dependable. They might be overly fond of wealth, and can have fairly conservative world views. Even in unhealthy or chaotic situations, they're able to bring along a more practical opinion.

Friends and Family

A home and family are two things that are important to a Taurus. Their sense of humor is good, and they're smart. This makes them great for socializing. They are also eager to help friends, and are loyal. Many of their friendships started as early as childhood.

Love and Sex

If you want to be a lover to a Taurus, you will need to be patient. Touch is an important thing to them, and they are very sensual. They tend to seek out partners who are from the same type of social circles, so they can share a desire for leisure and intellectual stimulation. They use material possessions and gifts to express their affection.

Gemini

Birth date range: May 20 - April 19
Element: Air
Planet: Mercury
Compatibility: Libra, Aquarius
Partnerships and marriage: Sagittarius

The symbol of the Gemini is two twins, each representing a dynamic side. This means people can't be sure which one they will interact with at any time. They're communicative, social, and often ready to have fun.

However, they can be equally thoughtful, serious, indecisive, and even restless.

An air sign, the Gemini will be interested with things to do with the mind. The ruling planet is Mercury, and it represents teaching other people, writing, and communicating. Just about everything in life is fascinating to them, and they will feel that there's not enough time to experience it all. Consequently, they can be brilliant writers, artists, or journalists.

Those born under the sign of the Gemini will feel that half of them is missing. They're always looking to rectify this emptiness, by seeking out new colleagues, friends, and mentors. They're inquisitive, fun-loving, versatile, and never boring to be around.

Friends and Family

Being very social, they always have plenty of friends, and strong bonds with family members. They look to be understood, and enjoy chatting with people. A Gemini will seek out people who can communicate clearly. They consider family to be important, especially with those who are similar to the Gemini. It is common for Gemini-born to be good friends with their siblings.

Love and Sex

Gemini are always after intellectual challenges, but also fun. As a lover, they can be very fiery. Touch is as important as communication, and combining those two things is the ultimate goal. They're eager to be flirtatious and ask questions. They also don't shy away from having different lovers, so they can find the best match.

Cancer

Birth date range: June 21 - July 22
Element: Water
Planet: Moon
Compatibility: Scorpio, Pisces
Partnerships and marriage: Capricorn

Cancers are vastly sentimental and intuitive, and also one of the most difficult signs to become acquainted with. Family and home are important to them, and they become highly attached to others. They are also empathetic, loyal, sensitive, and emotional. They will be able to understand the suffering of others.

The ruling planet for Cancer-born is the Moon, with all of the different lunar cycles and phases. This relates to their shifting emotions, and internal questioning. Being so sensitive, these things are hard for a Cancer to control, especially when they're young. These things also usually lead to swings in mood, rage, and selfish acts.

However, a Cancer will act to help other people avoid conflict. One of the most positive aspects of a Cancer is their strong determination. They might not have grand ambitions, but that is only because they are content with a peaceful home, and happy family. Often, they will treat their colleagues as family members.

Friends and Family

Those born as Cancers will be excellent parents. They work to preserve family memories, and are sentimental. This makes them eager to share their experiences with family members.

Love and Sex

As such an emotional zodiac sign, feelings are connected to romance for a Cancer. Many times, they will show signs of sensibility without needing to make an effort. They are also caring and gentle as lovers. When seeking a partner, they will look for someone who can understand them. People who are overly ambitious, or superficial, are not desirable for romance.

Leo

Birth date range: Just 23 - August 23
Element: Fire
Planet: Sun
Compatibility: Aries, Sagittarius
Partnerships and marriage: Aquarius

A Leo is a natural leader. They are creative, confident in themselves, dramatic, dominant, and hard to resist. Whatever they want to achieve is possible for a Leo, no matter what it is. As a fire sign, they enjoy life and look for good times. They can use their brains to work out tough problems, and don't mind taking the initiative in this regard. They can experience problems, where they might become arrogant, inflexible, and even lazy.

Friends and Family

Leo is the most generous of all the signs. They're loyal and faithful as friends, and work to help other people, even if it's difficult and time consuming. You can rely on a Leo, and they are strong. This star sign can find a way to appeal to almost any person. They are gracious and humble, and enjoy hosting celebrations and events. Since social interaction is part of their nature, they are not often alone.

A Leo will do anything necessary to protect their family, during good and bad times, and they're also proud.

Love and Sex

As a fire sign, Leos are sincere about their feelings, and very passionate. During sex, they can be energetic, fun, and even adventurous. For a Leo, there is a distinct difference between sex and love. They will look for parters who allow them to be the a leader, and independent. When seeking partners, they also want someone who's not self-aware, and with the same type of intellect as them. While they might seem a little greedy or careless, they are loyal, fun, and generous with partners.

Virgo

Birth date range: August 24 - September 22
Element: Earth
Planet: Mercury
Compatibility: Taurus, Capricorn
Partnerships and marriage: Pisces

Virgos are one of the more cautious of the signs. This is because they pay attention to tiny details, and have a strong sense of what humanity is about. They use method to figure life out, and dislike leaving things to chance.

As an Earth sign, Virgo-born seek organized and conservative things. While they are often organized with their lives, they can be messy. Either way, they like to clearly define their dreams and goals. The ruling planet for Virgos is Mercury, giving them a strong sense of communication, including writing and speech. They often seek careers as journalists and writers.

Friends and Family

Virgos make very useful friends. They give good advise, and solve problems well. Those born under this sign will remind their loved ones to look after themselves, since they focus heavily on wellness and health. They care about the sick and elderly, and remain dedicated to their families. They make superb parents, but are not the sort to openly tell others their feelings. A Virgo would rather show people through actions.

Love and Sex

Virgos need their partners to desire them. They are methodical, and tactical, so they make wonderful lovers. Even though they don't like to state their feelings of love directly, they will show them during sex. They only seek a handful of good relationships in their lives, instead of multiple partners. They're dedicated and faithful while in a relationship.

Libra

Birth date range: September 23 - October 22
Element: Air
Planet: Venus
Compatibility: Gemini, Aquarius
Partnerships and marriage: Aries

Those who are born under the sign of Libra despise being by themselves. They are fair and peaceful. Because they love cooperating with people, and being victorious together, they will always avoid being alone. As an air sign, they have keen intellects and enjoy deep discussions, good books, and fascinating people.

Venus is the ruling planet of Libra, and loves all things beautiful. They prefer qualify over quantify, and will tend to surround themselves with music, art, and beautiful environments.

Friend and Family

Libras are ever-ready to help others, and enjoy having fun. These attributes make them good friends. They might be indecisive, or create delays, but they are still truly wonderful friends. People want to have the company of Libra-born. They are loving, social, and understand what is required to create environments that everyone can enjoy.

They like to organize social gatherings, and love spending time with family and friends. They're good at sorting out disputes, and solving problems among others.

Love and Sex

A Libra wants to find the right partner, and makes this a priority. If they are in a relationship, keeping the harmony is vital for them. They feel unnatural with being alone, and it makes them very sad. They're expressive, balanced, and creative lovers, willing to do what it takes to make their partner happy. With their dedication, and sense of charm, they are excellent romantic partners.

Scorpio

Birth date range: October 24 - November 22
Element: Water
Planet: Pluto
Compatibility: Cancer, Pisces
Partnerships and marriage: Taurus

Scorpios are assertive and passionate individuals. They will keep looking for answers, until the truth is found. This ties into their decisive and determined natures. Scorpio-born make excellent leaders, and will stay aware of what's happening around them. Resourcefulness is another strong characteristic of those born under the sign of the Scorpio.

As a water sign, they want to express their feelings, and experience things. However, they don't show their emotions in the same way as other water signs. If you tell a Scorpio a secret, they will always keep it private.

Friends and Family

Two things that make Scorpios good friends are their fairness and honesty. When it comes to work, they're loyal and dedicated. They have quick wits, and are intelligent, so they look for similar people. A love of fun is also a trait that they look for in friends. They will give you anything you want or need, but will not forgive you if you let them down.

Love and Sex

This is the most sensual out of all the zodiac signs. They're overtly intimate and passionate, and these things are important to a Scorpio. For partners, they look for honesty and intelligence. After they fall in love with someone, A Scorpio-born is totally faithful and dedicated. Since it can take a lot of time for them to build up trust in partnerships, they are careful about choosing the right people.

Sagittarius

Birth date range: November 23 - December 21
Element: Fire
Planet: Jupiter
Compatibility: Aries, Leo
Partnerships and marriage: Gemini

A Sagittarius will be energetic and curious. They love to travel more than most other signs. They have strong philosophical views, and open minds, which encourage them to wander and look for meaning in life.

Sagittarius-born are optimistic, extroverted, enthusiastic, and enjoy change. They can fulfill their goals, because of an ability to turn thoughts into actions. As with all fire signs, those born under this sign long to be connected with the world. Their ruling planet is Jupiter, which is the biggest of the planets in the zodiac. They have boundless enthusiasm, and also strong senses of humor.

Friends and Family

They are constantly with friends, and are fun to about around. They enjoy experiencing diverse cultures, and making friends with people from all around the planet. They're generous, and avoid lecturing others. They're willing to do what it takes to look after family, and also enjoy laughing.

Love and Sex

Being humorous and playful, they like to have fun with with partners. If they find someone who's just as open, the relationship will blossom. A Sagittarius suits someone who is expressive, passionate, and willing to try just about anything.

Capricorn

Birth date range: December 22 - January 20
Element: Earth
Planet: Saturn
Compatibility: Taurus, Virgo
Partnerships and marriage: Cancer

Capricorns hold onto traditional values, and are the most professional of the signs. They are also the most serious sign, and are practical people. Their strong independence makes it possible for them to develop themselves greatly, both on a personal and business level.

Being an earth sign, Capricorns value family over anything else. They are experts at self-control, and might be strong leaders in the area of business. Capricorn's ruling planet is Saturn, which signifies restriction. This makes them responsible and practical, so they're able to save money. They might be stubborn, and looking to prove they are right. However, this can help them to be the best at many things.

Friend and Family

Being funny and intelligent, it's easy for Capricorns to make good friends. They expect their friends to be loyal and honest. With family, as well as friends, they don't have any boundaries. They view family traditional as important, and love to spend special holidays together. They're prone to expressing themselves through bursts of emotion.

Love and Sex

It can be hard to win the favor of a Capricorn. If someone does manage to form a relationship with one, they will be committed to that person for life. They are serious as lovers, and enjoy doing things thoroughly, and slowly. They use actions to express their feelings, instead of words. They will happily spend money on their partner, and are caring and loyal.

Conclusion

Once you start to understand more about astrology, and how many people enjoy following it, you will quickly realize why it's so popular. You can save yourself a lot of time and worry, by thinking about what the future might hold for you. This in turn gives you time to make decisions about how you can improve your life. This type of self-reflection is essential for all people, if they want to lead fulfilling and productive lives.

Even if you don't believe that astrology has any grounding in reality or science — it can just be a whole lot of fun. All of the different zodiac signs, dates, and the special little fortune telling techniques, are very appealing. No matter what type of information you find out, it can be related to different aspects of your life.

Made in the USA
Middletown, DE
12 November 2015